Speak (khu-luma) Siswati

by Phelelisiwe Dlamini

Speak (Khu-luma) Siswati
Copyright © 2021 by Phelelisiwe Dlamini

All rights reserved. No part of this publication
may be reproduced, distributed, or
transmitted in any form or by any means,
including photocopying, recording, or
other electronic or mechanical methods,
without the prior written permission of
the author, except in the case of brief
quotations embodied in critical reviews
and certain other non-commercial
uses permitted by copyright law.

Tellwell Talent
www.tellwell.ca

ISBN
978-0-2288-4556-0 (Paperback)
978-0-2288-4557-7 (eBook)

Dedication...

This book is dedicated to my children, Bandile Phiri and Daliso Phiri. I hope one day you will be able to communicate using Siswati, this language is part of your genes and you should be proud and honoured to be part of the Swati people of the Kingdom of Eswatini

Introduction

Siswati is the native language of the Kingdom of eSwatini (formally known as Swaziland). It is a small Kingdom in Southern Africa at the bottom tip of Mozambique and boarded by South Africa.

Introduction

This book is written for beginners and other new comers to the Siswati language

Siswati is a slow spoken language. in order to learn it well, the slower you are in pronouncing every vowel, the better you will be in speaking it.

There is a saying in Eswatini that "there is no hurry in Swaziland", this exemplifies in the spoken language.

The most common error people make when learning to speak Siswati is to rush their words. The best way to learn the Siswati language is to get your speech sounds right. If a learner can slow down and ensure that they are pronouncing sounds correctly, they will find it easier to advance in the language.

The secret is....imagine an accent on every vowel, pronounce and stress every vowel.

Introduction

I am inspired to teach you how to speak and read Siswati as it is mostly spoken in the present time, using a lot of english words, this will make it somehow easier.

There are two official languages in Eswatini. Siswati and English. Most people can understand both clearly, the majority of young people, can understand, speak and write clearly in both languages. Although majority of the time you will find them speaking in Siswati because they are proud to be Swati.

As such, the Siswati original language has greatly changed to include a lot of English in it. If you are an English Speaker, you are at a great advantage because you can include a lot of English words to merge into speaking Siswati.

The secret is....imagine an accent on every vowel, pronounce and stress every vowel.

Introduction

Keep repeating, keep repeating........ saying the words out loud.

Try to accomplish learning something new everyday.

Spend time in the kingdom of Eswatini (Swaziland).

If you are lucky enough to be around Siswati speaking people, practise as often as possible by listening and asking people to slow down and repeat, speak in Siswati to them, not english.

The secret is....imagine an accent on every vowel, pronounce and stress every vowel.

THE VOWELS

a, e, i, o, u

Any first learner should start with the vowels;

a   said as in the first 'a' in the word 'apple' in English

e   said as in the first 'e' in the word 'enter' in English

i   said as in the first 'i' in the word 'ink' in english

o   said as in the first 'o' in the word 'oven' in english

u   said as in the word 'lucy' in English, say the word 'Lucy' without the 'L' then practice saying the word 'lucy' without the 'l,c & y''

The secret is....imagine an accent on every vowel, pronounce and stress every vowel.

THE ALPHABET

Learning the alphabet is the second most important thing in learning siSwati

This is the alphabet in siSwati from A to C

A said as in the first 'a' in the word 'apple' in English

B said as in the 'ba' in basement, bathing 'lets try saying it with the vowels - ba, be, bi, bo, bu

C This is the click sound!!!
I couldn't really find an equivalent for this sound in English - so I will teach you how to do it with your tough. Open the mouth like you are saying 'a' as in 'apple', then stick your tough to the top of the roof of your mouth, include a little sucking motion, then with a push forward motion of your tough, snap your tough down from the roof to about the middle of your mouth, this is the sound of C

THE ALPHABET

Learning the alphabet is the second most important thing in learning siSwati

This is the alphabet in siSwati from D to K

- D — Said as in the 'd' in diver
- E — the first 'e' in 'enter'
- F — the 'f' in 'father'
- G — the 'g' in the name 'Lady Gaga''
- H — the first 'h' in 'half'
- I — the first 'i' in 'ink'
- J — the first 'j' in 'jelly
- K — the 'c' in 'cabbage'

THE ALPHABET

Learning the alphabet is the second most important thing in learning siSwati

This is the alphabet in siSwati from L to S

L   Said as in the 'L' in the name "Lilly"

M   the 'm' in 'Mama''

N   the 'N' in 'November'

O   the 'O' in 'oven'

P   the 'P' in 'Peter''

Q   hardly used in Siswati

R   hardly used in Siswati

S   the 'S' in 'Sally''

THE ALPHABET

Learning the alphabet is the second most important thing in learning siSwati

This is the alphabet in siSwati from T to Z

T   Said as 'T' in "tata'

U   Say the name 'Lucy' in english, say it without the 'L', then practice saying the name 'Lucy' without the 'L,C & Y'

V   the 'V' in 'Volleyball'or 'Vent''

W   the 'W' in 'Wall' or 'wallet'

X   Another click sound! say it like the letter 'C

Y   the 'y' in 'yam' ' yahtzee' 'yellow'

Z   the 'Z' in 'Zee' or 'Zebra'

A - apple

Li - hhabhula
ema - hhabhula (plural)

B - Bee

I - Nyosi
Ti - Nyosi (plural)

C - cow

I - nkhomo
Ti - nkhomo (Plural)

D - dancing

Ngiya - jayiva (I am)
uya - jayiva (she/he is)
siya - jayiva (we are)
baya - jayiva (they are)

E - egg

li-candza
ema - candza (plural)

F - Fire

um-lilo
imi - lilo (plural)

G - garden

i - ngadze
ti- ngadze (plural)

House
i -ndlu
ti-ndlu (plural)

I Inside

Ekhatsi

J Jam

Jamu

K King
i-nkhosi
Ema-khosi (plural)

L

Ngiya-hleka (I am - Laughing)
uyahleka (she/he)
bayahleka (they are)
uhlekani ? (What are you laughing at ?)
uhlekisa - making fun of

Laugh - Hleka

Mother

Make - wami (my mother)
Make - wakho (your mother)
Make - wakhe (her/his mother)
Make - wabo (their mother)

N - for no
cha

O for Owl
Sikhova - tikhova

P for pee
kuchama

Q for Queen
indlovukati

R for Run
Gijima

S for stand up
sukuma

S for sit
hlala
hlala-phansi (sit down)
hlala - esitulweni (sit on the chair)

T FOR TELEPHONE
LUCINGO
OR
I - CELL PHONE

U FOR UNDERWEAR
I-PENTI (WOMEN'S UNDERWEAR)
I- UNDER (MEN'S UNDERWEAR)

V FOR VEGETABLES
EMA-VEGETABLES

W FOR WALK
HAMBA
KU-HAMBA

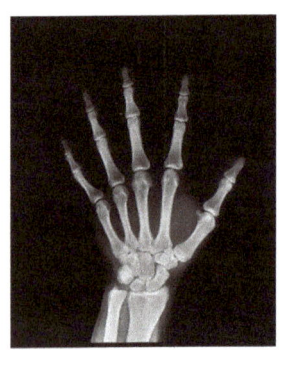

X FO X-RAY
I-XRAY

Y FOR YES
YEBO

Z FOR ZEBRA
I-ZEBRA

THE SIGNATURE SISWATI SOUND

---

tsa tse tsi tso tsu

The Zulu language, which is the closest language to Siswati says'
za ze zi zo zu
ema - swati say'
tsa tse tsi tso tsu

Learn to say this sound and you will be sounding like an original in no time!

Try pushing air out of your mouth like you were using your mount to spray water (teeth clenched) ....

this is .....tse

tsa - you drop the mount open a little
tse - you spay water
tsi - you spray water more intensely
tso - you spray water with a round mouth
tsu - you spray water with a duck mount

Making Words with Vowels and the Alphabet

la le li lo lu
na ne ni no nu
ma me mi mo mu
kha khe khi kho khu

kha - said as in the first "co" in the word "come"

khe - said as in the first "ca" in the word "cake"

khi - said as in the word "key"

kho - said as in the first "co" in "cop"

khu - said as in the word "coup" which means a highly successful, act or move, a clever action or accomplishment.

Making Words with Vowels and the Alphabet

va ve vi vo vu
sa se si so su
ba be bi bo bu
ca ce ci co cu

go through the alphabet and make up your own combinations with the vowels and letters, and make the 'a,e,i,o,u" combinations, say them out loud.

Even though this exercise is a bit boring because you keep repeating things and you have no clue what they mean. The time you invest in this exercise will benefit you greatly in advancing to the next level, where we will start learning what words mean as we will now be in a a better position to not only sound out the word, but know its meaning, so that when we hear it being sounded out by other people, we will know what it means.

Making Words with Vowels and the Alphabet

nga nge ngi ngo ngu

To sound out this combination is important to learn as it is used often in speaking Siswati

ngi - means "I am"

ngu - means "he is" "she is"

It is a unique sound but I think this is how you try it as a non siswati speaker;

when you say the vowel "a" you push the air out of your mouth, try saying "a" but pulling the air inward and dropping the trout muscles lower to create a bigger opening.

this should produce the sound 'nga'

Essential Siswati Phrases

SISWATI	ENGLISH
ikuphi – i – toilet	Where is the bathroom?
Mani	stop
hamba	go
ngilambile	I am hungry
ngicela	please
ngicela emanti	please, water
kum-nandzi	its delicious
Malini?	how much?

Essential Siswati Phrases

SISWATI	ENGLISH
sawubona (sanibonani - plural)	hello
ngiyacela (siyacela - plural)	please
ngiyabonga (siyabonga - plural)	Thank you
Hamba - kahle	go well (bye)
sala - kahle	saty well (bye)
unjani (ninjani - plural)	how are you?
yebo	yes
cha	no

Siswati relationships

ENGLISH	SISWATI
Mother (Mom)	Make
father (Dad)	Babe
Wife	Umfati
Husband	indzodza
child	umftwana
My child	umftwanami
Your child	umftwanakho
Sister	Sisi
Brother	Bhuti
uncle (Mother's brother)	Malume
Aunt (Father's Sister)	Anti

Siswati relationships

ENGLISH	SISWATI
Aunt (Mother's older sister)	Make- lomkhulu (Mom-mkhulu) meaning - big mother)
Aunt (Mother's younger sister)	Make-lomcane (Mom-mcane) (small mother)
Aunt (Uncle's wife)	Malume (called the same as the male side of the relationship)
Cousin	Mzala
Teacher	Thishela
Pastor (minister)	Umfundzisi

KUDLA - FOOD

SALAD - ISALAD
RICE - IRICE
SOUP - ISOUP
MEAT - INYAMA
FRUTS - EMA-FRUITS
BANANA - BANANA
APPLE - LIHHABHULA
TOMATOE - LITAMATISI
SPINACH - SPINACH

COLORS: EMA COLORS

RED - BOVU
BLUE - HLATA
GREEN - LOKU-GREEN
YELLOW - LOKU-YELLOW
WHITE - LOKU-MHLOPHE

YOU CAN USE "LOKU......" FOR A LOT OF COLORS, JUST ADD ENGLISH COLOR NAME LOKU-PURPLE.

SOME WORDS IN ENGLISH CAN BE USED IN SISWATI

Tilwane - Animals

SISWATI	ENGLISH
Libhubesi (emabhubesi) - plural	Lion (s)
Zebra (ema zebra)	Zebra (s)
Inyoka (Tinyoka)	Snake (s)
Inyoni (Tinyoni)	Bird (s)
Indlovu (Tindlovu)	Elephant (s)
Inkhomo (Tinkhomo)	Cow (s)

Inkhukhu (Tinkhukhu)	Chicken (s)
Imbhuti (Timbhuti)	Goat (s)
Lihhashi (emahhashi)	Horse (s)

THE FACE

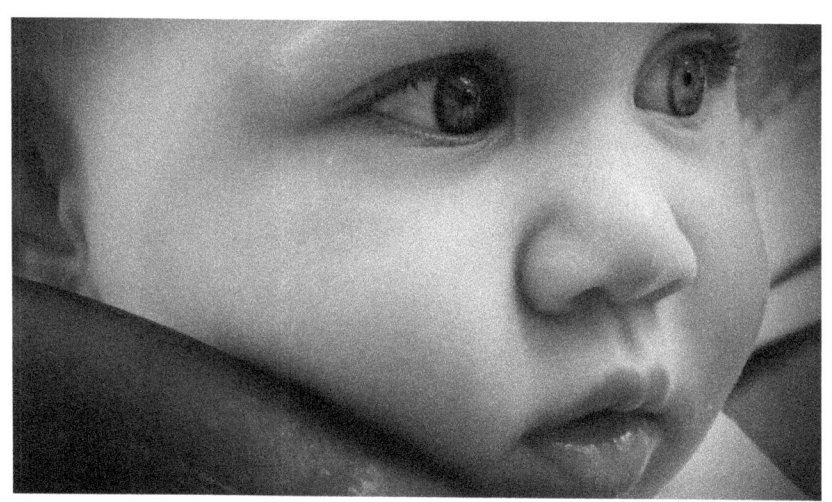

SISWATI	ENGLISH
Buso	face
Liso - emehlo (plural)	eye - eyes
likhala - emakhala	nose
umlomo - imilomo	mouth
indlebe - tindlebe	ear - ears
sihlatsi - tihlatsi	cheek (s)
emashiya	eye-lashes
ematse	saliva
umphefumulo	breath (life)
tinyembheti	tears

The Body

SISWATI	ENGLISH
umtimbha	body
inhloko - tinhloko	head - heads
tinwele	hair
intsamo - tintsamo	neck - necks
umkhono -imikhono	arm - arms
sandla - tandla	hand - hands
sifuba - tifuba	chest - chests
sisu - tisu	stomach (s)
sibunu -tibunu	buttocks (bum)
inhlitiyo - tinhlitiyo	heart - hearts

THE BODY

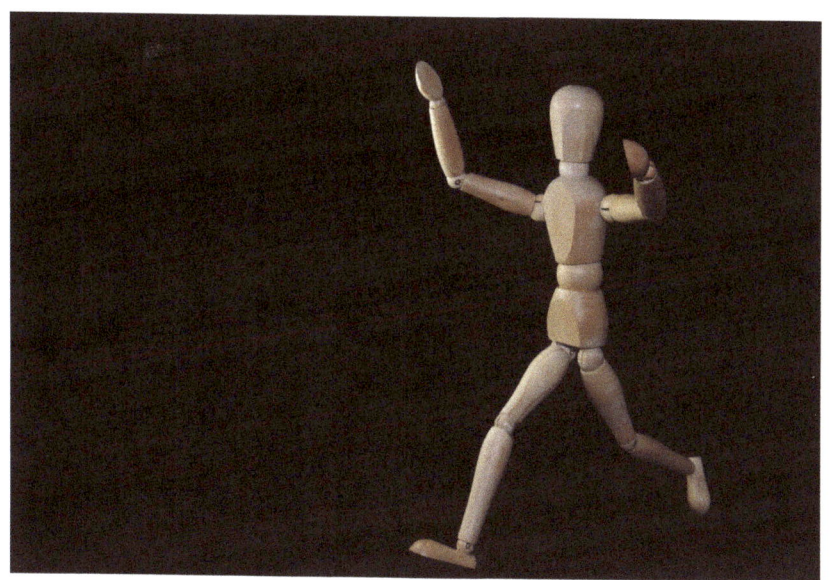

SISWATI

umlente - imilente
lumyawo - tinyawo
lugalo (tingalo)
likhwapha (emakhwapha)
Litsanga (ematsanga)

The same word - litsanga - is used for pumpkin in siswati!!
Litsanga - ematsanga

ENGLISH

leg - legs
foot - feet
nail (nails)
armpit (armpits)
thigh (thighs)

pumpkin - (s)

OUTSIDE

SISWATI	ENGLISH
sibhakabhaka	sky
Lifu - emafu	Cloud (s)
tjani	grass
litje - ematje	stone (s)
sihlahla - tihlahla	tree (s)
intsaba - tintsaba	mountain (s)
umfula - imifula	river (s)
imbhali - timbhali	flower (s)
lilanga	sun
inyeti	moon

OUTSIDE

SISWASTI	ENGLISH
Umhlabatsi	soil
unhlaba	planet earth
licembhe (emacembhe)	leaf - leaves
inkhanyeti (tinkhanyeti)	star (s)

Weather

SISWATI	ENGLISH
Libalele	clear skies
liyashisa or kuyashisa	sunny (hot)
liyana or kunemvula	raining
linile	it rained
litulu (kind of means up)	rain
lisibekele	cloudy
sangcotfo	hail
liyakhifitela	drizzling
lidzaka	mud
kuyashelela	slippery
kumakhata	cold
kune-sitfwatfwa	there is - frost
iyeta - imvula or liyeta-litulu	rain is coming
liyadvuma	thunder

EMOTIONS IN SISWATI

SISWATI	ENGLISH
kuhleka	to laugh
ngiya - hleka	I am laughing
baya - hleka	they are laughing
uya - hleka	she/he is laughing
uhleka - bani?	who are you laughing at?
bahleka - bani?	who are they laughing at?
uhlekani?	what are you laughing at?
uyakuhleka..	she/he is laughing at you.
bayakuhleka...	they are laughing at you.
baya-hlekana	They laugh at people
baku - hlekile	they laughed at you
batoku - hleka	they will laugh at you

EMOTIONS IN SISWATI

SISWATI	ENGLISH
kukhala	to cry
ngiyakhala	I am crying
uyakhaya	she/he is crying
bayakhala	they are crying
ngikhalile	I cried
bakhalile	they cried
ukhalelani?	what are you crying for?
Bakhalelani?	what are they crying for?
uyam-khalisa	you are making she/he cry
umkhalise- lani?	why are you making she/he cry?
ngiyakukhalela	I am crying for you (feel sorry for you)
ngiyabakhalela	I am crying for them (feel sorry for them)

Emotions in Siswati

SISWATI	ENGLISH
Thula	quiet
ngithulile	I am quiet
uthulile	she/he is quiet
bathulile	they are quiet
uthuleleni?	why are you quiet?
bathulise	make them be quiet
nginemahloni	I am shy
unemahloni	she/he is shy
banemahloni	they are shy
uyaphapha	she/he is too lively (annoying way)
uyangi-phaphela	she/he is annoying me

KITCHEN

SISWATI	ENGLISH
indishi – tindishi	dish (bowl)(s)
Lipledi – ema pledi	plate(s)
isinki	sink
impompi – timpompi	tap(s)
litafula – ema tafula	table(s)
situlo – titulo	chair(s)
i-avini – ema avini	oven(s)
sipunu – tipunu	spoon(s)
i-fork –ema forks	fork(s)
libhodzo – ema bhodzo	pot(s)
umukhwa (umese) – imikhwa	knife(s)
sitofu – titofu	stove(s)
i-fridge – emafridge	fridge(s)
si spice – ema spices	spice(s)
swayi	salt
shukela	sugar
ligedlela	kettle
i-dish washer	dish washer

Kitchen

SISWATI	ENGLISH
emanti	water
ifasitela	window
umtsanyelo	broom
i-mop	mop
libhakede	bucket
i-dust bin	dust bin
gesi	gas
likhuni- tinkhuni	firewood
tinsaba	kindling
imlilo	fire
sitofu	stove
umlotsa	ash

SISWATI	ENGLISH
Hlabela	Sing
kuhlabela	to sing
ngiya-hlabela	I am singing
uya-hlabela	she/he is singing
baya-hlabela	They are singing
ngihlabelile	I sang
uhlabelile	she/he sang
bahlabelile	they sang
um-hlabeleli	singer
ba-hlabeleli	singers

SISWATI

Jayiva
kujayiva
ngiya-jayiva
uya-jayiva

baya-jayiva
ngijayivile
ujayivile
bajayivile
um-jayivo
um-jayivi
ba-jayivi

ENGLISH

Dance
to dance
I am dancing
she/he is dancing

They are dancing
I danced
she/he danced
they danced
the dance
the dancer
dancers

DATES

namuhla	Today
itolo	yesterday
Kusasa	Tomorrow
liviki	Week
liviki - leliphelile	last week (literal translation - the week that has finished)
liviki - lelitako	next week (literal translation -the week that is coming)
inyanga	Month
inyanga -lephelile	last month
inyamga letako	next month
Um-nyaka	Year

! inyanga also means traditional medicine doctor!!

Short Conversation Stories

Morning greeting - Siswati and English

Sawubona
hello

unjani? ulele-njani?
how are you? how did you sleep?

sitodlani? for i-breakfast?
what will we eat for breakfast?

angati
I dont know

u suggester ini?
what do you suggest?

Litiya? licoffee?
tea? coffee?

kute litiya
there is no tea

kunelicoffee kuphela
there is coffee only

Short Conversation Stories

Morning greeting
Siswati and English literal translation

Sawubona
I see you

unjani? ulele-njani?
how are you? you slept how?

sitodlani? for i-breakfast?
what will we eat? for breakfast?

a-ngati
I dont know

u suggester ini?
you suggest what?

Litiya? licoffee?
tea? coffee?

kute litiya
There is no tea

kunelicoffee kuphela
there is coffee only

Short Conversation Stories

Asking for direction

You:
Ncesi - Sisi (Bhuti,Make,Babe)
excuse me - Sister (Brother, Mother, Father)

Note to visually by age figure out someone's age, compared to your age. This is Siswati respect and people appreciate it.

The other:
Yebo
Yes?
if they respect you as well, they will say Yebo - sisi etc.

You:
Ngingayitsengaphi i air-time?
Where can I buy air-time?

The other:
itsengiswa lapha.....pointing most likely
they sell it there.....

You:
Ngiyabonga
Thank you.

Short Stories

John's new wallet

One sunny morning,

ekuseni libalele,

as John got out of bed and made his way into the kitchen,

wavuka John waya ekhishini,

he was greeted by mother who was cooking his favourite breakfast dish.

Wam-bingelela wake wakhe, apheka kudla kwasekuseni kwakhe lakakutsandza kakhulu

"Sour porridge! Thank you Mother!"

incwancwa! ngi - yabonga Make!

"You are welcome John."

kute inkinga (no problem)

Mother placed a bowl of hot porridge on the table for John.

Make wabeka incwancwa ya-John etafuleni

SHORT STORIES

John's new wallet

John used a spoon to eat his porridge.

Wadla incwancwa yakhe ngesipunu John

The porridge tasted delicious and for this, John was happy.

ingasem-nandzi incwancwa, yamu jabulisa John.

As John ate his porridge mother put a black wallet on the table next to him.

asadla John, wabeka sipatji lesimnyama etafuleni eceleni kwa John Make wakhe.

"Mother, what is this?" John asked.

yini lena Make?

"This is a wallet John. It's used to hold your money."

yi wallet John, esetjentiswa kufaka imali John.

Short Stories

John's new wallet

"Why would i want the wallet to hold my money?"

ngitoyentani mine i wallet kefaka imali?

"So that it doesn't get lost."

Khona ingato lahleka imali yakho

"I understand."

ngiyeva (i hear)

John examined the black wallet carefully.

wayibuka wayi-bukisisa i-wallet John

"Mother?" asked John,

Make?

"Yes John?"

Yebo John

Short Stories

                                                  John's new wallet

"I don't have any money to put in my wallet."

Ngite imali lengitayifaka ku-wallet yami

Mother smiled and pulled from her pocket two 100 rand bills.

wa si-miler Make wakhe, wakhipha 2 wema ma 100 emalangeni bills ekhikhini

"Here you are John. 200 Rands for your wallet."

naku John, 200 emalangeni e wallet yakho

"Hwu Make, that's too much money for me.

"Hwu make" imali lenengi kangaka!

"I want you to take the bus to your grandmother's house this afternoon.

ngifuna ugibele ibhasi uye kagogo entsambhama

Short Stories

John's new wallet

At grandmother's house you will pick ripe peaches to bring back to me so that i can make your favorite dessert."

nawifika kagogo, ukhe emampentjisa lavutsiwe ubuye nawo ngitopheka i-dessert kakho loyitsandzako

"Peach pie!" John shouted with joy.

i-peach pie! washo ngenjabulo John.

John finished his porridge and got ready to go to Grandmother's house.

wacedza kudla John walungisela kuya kagogo

Short Stories

                              John' rides the kumbie

To get to the bus station, John must first ride the kumbie into town.

Kuya esiteshini se bhasi, kufanele agibele i kumbie aye edolobheni John.

John waits for the kumbie with Mother.

Wamela i kumbie esiteshini na Make wake John

John is carrying his backpack and inside his backpack is everything he needs for his trip:

Uphatse ngabhaki wake konkhe lakudzingako

his water bottle,

Libhodlela lake lemanti

his bags for carrying Khokho's peaches

Sikhwama sekuphatsa emampentjisa

And of course, his new black wallet.

ne wallet yakhe

Short Stories

John' rides the kumbie

When the kumbie arrives John says "Goodbye" to mother.
"Goodbye John. I will see you in the evening."

nayifika i kumbie wavalelisa Make wakhe

"hamba kahle John, ngitakubona entsambhama."

"Where are you going John?"

uyaphi ye John?

"I am going to the bus station!"

ngiya esiteshini

"And where are you taking the bus to?"

ugibela i bus uyaphi?

"I am going to Khokho's house in Nhlangano!"

ngiya ka Khokho e Nhlangano

Short Stories

John' rides the kumbie

John had taken the kumbie many times before with mother.

akacali kugibela i - kumbie John, uhlala ayigibela na make wakhe.

He knew that when the kumbie approached the bus station he needed to say "stop" so that the driver knew when he needed to get out.

uyati kutsi nase itofika esiteshini sakhe kufanele amemete atsi "stesh" "or Mani" atokwati umshayeli kutsi ufuna kwehla John.

During the ride to town, John stared out the window determined not to miss his stop.

e kumbhini wabuka ngelifasitelo John angafuni simengce siteshi.

Through the window John could see all sorts of things:

ngeli fasitelo wabona tintfo letinengi

Short Stories

John' rides the kumbie

Children playing with a ball,

Bantfwana badlala ngebhola

Grandmothers walking slowly up the road

bo Gogo bahambha kancane engwacweni

Trees swaying in the soft African wind.

tihlahla it tishaywa ngumoya , umoya we Africa

As the kumbie rolled into town John saw the gas station pass by.

Nayingena edolobheni i kumbie, wabona i gas station yengca

He saw people carrying grocery bags to their cars.

Wabona bantfu ba tfwele ema grocery bags balayisha etimotweni tabo

And finally, he saw the bus station.
"Stop!!!!"

Short Stories

John' rides the kumbie

And finally, he saw the bus station.

abona i bus station

"Stop!!!!"

Stesh!!!!

IN THE KITCHEN

a random conversation

Hey!
yebo!

what are you doing?
wentani?

I'm cooking
ngiya-pheka

what are you cooking?
uphekani?

i'm making chiken
ngi pheka inkhukhu

with what?
nani?

and rice
ne rice

IN THE KITCHEN

---

a random conversation

Hey!
yebo!

can I help?
ngicela kusita

you can clean the table
unga cleana litafula

and wash the dishes
ugeze netitja

so much work!
umsebenti longaka!

you are lazy
uyavilapha

im lot lazy, im tired
angi vilaphi, ngi dziniwe

IN THE KITCHEN

a random conversation

Hello!
sawubona! or sanibonani!

I am dying of cold!
ngiyafa nge makhata
pronounce (ngi as ni - to start)
pronounce (kha as ca)

the fire is hot! its nice!
uya shisa um lilo! um nandzi!
pronounce (ndzi as ndi - to start)

let me sit down next to it
ase ngi hlale la e celeni kwawo

put some more wood in the fire
faka ti - nkhuni kulo mlilo

play some music on your phone
dlala u music ku cell phone yakho

OUT

---

a random conversation

Yebo!
Hello....but really meaning "yes"!

how are you?
unjani?

uwakuphi wena?
where are you from?

ngi wa la
I am from here

unemanga!
you are lying

wena uwakuphi?
you...where are you from?

ekhaya kuse Nhlangano
my home is in nhlangano

where is that?
kukuphi lapho

2 hours u driver
2 hours if driving

KUSOMA

a random conversation

greeting:
Yebo bhuti/sisi/babe/make
hello brother/sister/dad/mom

Flurting:
whats your name
ungu bani ligama lakho

why are you asking
ubute lani?

I just want to get to know you
ngifuna kukwati

umuhle
you look beautiful

leave me alone
awungi yekele

ngicela i cell phone number
can i have your cell phone numbner

SHOPPING

a random conversation

hello
sawubona

how much are the apples/banana
malini lihhabhula/banana

10 emalangeni/5 emalangeni

can i have two of them
ngicela lamabili or ngicela two

do you sell tomatoes?
uyawa tsengisa ema tamatisi?

no i dont sell them
anginawo

banawo lapha
they have them over there

thanks
ngiya bonga

VOICE RECORDINGS

VISIT AUTHOR WEBSITE

a random conversation

I understand that learning Siswati can be greatly enhanced if you can hear it voiced out

please visit my author website for voice recordings of the book

www.ingramcontent.com/pod-product-compliance
Lightning Source LLC
LaVergne TN
LVHW072023060526
838200LV00058B/4656